# I Know My ZBCs

## 59 SCHOOL POEMS FOR YOUNG GIGGLERS

by
# Ted Scheu

photographs by
## Peter Lourie

Young
Poets'
Press

MIDDLEBURY, VT

*With deepest thanks to a bunch of wonderfully energetic and photogenic first graders at the Sustainability Academy at Lawrence Barnes in Burlington, VT, and their dedicated teachers, parents, and marvelous principal, Abi Sessions. Thanks also to a gaggle of gregariously gorgeous young friends in Middlebury, VT—all of whom also seriously hammed it up for Pete's camera. Hopefully you all had fun!*

*Very special additional thanks to two extra-amazing classes of first and second graders and their super-duper teachers, who helped me immeasurably by honestly sharing their opinions of the poems early in the process: Sally Stevens and her super-cool Kaleidoscope class at the Shelburne Community School in Shelburne, VT; and Judy McBride and her awesome class at the Katonah Elementary School in Katonah, NY. You are the best!*

*And, of course, I always need to thank four more folks: my most-marvelously patient and supportive wife, Robin; Angie Wiechmann, my editor extraordinaire, for her talented eyes, ears and heart; my ever-inspiring friend and photographer, Pete Lourie; and, last but not least, Win Colwell for his always-brilliant designs, his fortitude, and his friendship.*

**Now I Know My ZBCs**
First Edition, November 2011

Text copyright © 2011 by Ted Scheu
Photographs copyright © 2011 by Peter Lourie
Design by Winslow Colwell/WColwell Design

Published in the United States by Young Poets' Press
PO Box 564, Middlebury, VT 05753
www.youngpoetspress.com

For further information, or to reproduce selections from this book, write to
Young Poets' Press
PO Box 564, Middlebury, VT 05753

The text of this publication was set in American Typewriter.

ISBN 978-0-9825499-4-0
Library of Congress Control Number: 2011935710

This collection is dedicated with love and thanks to my amazing mom, to the memory of my remarkable dad, and to my other early teachers, all of whom worked hard to teach me my ZBCs.

# Table of Contents

# My Mirror Really Likes Me

My mirror really likes me.
I guess it's no surprise.
I saw a spark of friendship
just this morning in his eyes.

When I woke up, he greeted me
as I was standing there.
We smiled at each other,
and he really seemed to care.

I told him he was looking good.
He said the same to me.
I've never had a friend with whom
I've talked so easily.

He looks a little like me
and moves the same way, too.
He wears my same pajamas,
and he sneezes like I do.

It could be just coincidence—
or lucky, I suppose—
but when I winked, he did the same,
and then we picked our nose.

Though we're alike, there are a couple
differences I spied.
I saw, like me, he'd lost a tooth,
but on the other side.

I waved goodbye and caught the bus.
And later it was cool—
I noticed, in the bathroom,
he had followed me to school.

## Disappointment

The bouncy balls are waiting
in their basket by the door.
The jump ropes lurk like eager snakes
in coils on the floor.

A box of cones and bases
is sitting patiently,
and coats and outdoor voices
are longing to be free.

Above it all, a cloud has formed
that's deep and dark and wide.
The principal has just announced
that recess is *inside*.

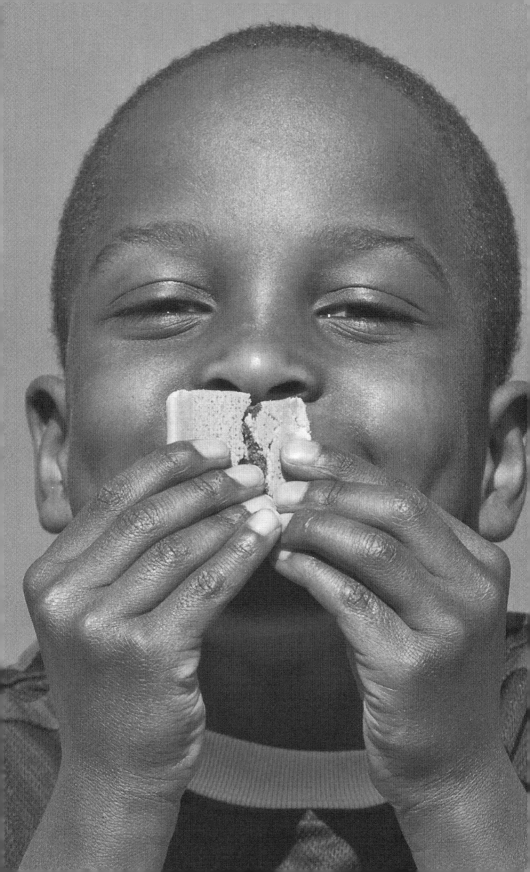

## Snack Magic

Because we're friends, I'll share with you
a trick that I have found.
I use it every day at school
when snack time comes around.

Since I am always hungry,
I use my magic touch.
I break my cookie right in two
so I have *twice* as much!

# Teddy Bear Day

It's Teddy Bear Day today at school,
and everybody brought one.
But I said I like *real* bears,
so I went out and caught one.

He's pretty big and hairy,
like wild bears should be.
But my bear's not too scary,
and he's very fond of me.

He gives me hugs and rarely growls,
so I am super glad
that this year I have brought to school
my teddy bear of a dad.

## I'm *Not* Free!

In school today, I realized
I'm very proud to be
living in a country
where everyone is free.

I told my little sister this—
she scowled and slammed the door.
I heard her say as she stomped away,
"I'm not *free*! I'm four!"

# How You Can Be as Smart as Me

I love learning,
yes sirree.
I know that one plus one
makes *three*!

Hey, I'm the smartest
kid alive.
I'm sure that two and two
is *five*!

Subtracting's also
lots of fun.
If you take two from four
it's *one*!

In spelling, too,
I am a star.
I see that *c-a-t*
spells *car*!

My brain's the brightest
I have found.
The squares I draw
are extra *round*!

You may not think
this stuff is true.
It is, and here's
what you can do:

If you play video games all day
and also watch TV,
someday, with lots of work and luck,
you'll be as smart as me!

# I Raised My Hands

I raised my hand in class today
because I thought I knew
exactly what and why and where
and when and how and who.

I threw another hand up high
to make my teacher see
that she could call on me and get
the answer easily.

She didn't seem to notice,
so I waved *another* hand.
I thought that having *three* arms up
would help her understand.

But three hands didn't seem to help,
so up flew number *four*.
Then *five* and *six* soon joined the fun,
like all my arms before.

My final chance was *seven* and *eight*;
I waved them frantically.
At last, my teacher seemed to see—
she turned and called on me.

Today I learned a simple truth
I shouldn't have to mention:
It helps to be an octopus
to get someone's attention.

**Now I Know My ZBCs**
*(Sing to the tune of "The Alphabet Song")*

Z-B-C-D, Q-H-P,
R-Y-W-X, S-U-V,
A-F-L, K-O-E,
M-G-N, I-J-T.

Now I know my ZBCs—
the alphabet for chimpanzees.

15

## Nancy Cristman Kissed Me

Nancy Cristman kissed me
as we walked to school today.
It happened fast, and I was lost
with what to do or say.

I quickly looked around to check
if anyone had seen it.
If they did, and tease me,
they'll be sorry—and I mean it.

Why did Nancy Cristman put
that smack upon my cheek?
I'm so confused and probably
will stay this way all week.

I'll guess I'll have to marry her
and share my lemonade.
A lot can happen to a kid
who walks to second grade.

## I Made Some Great Connections

Each day in school, I try to make
a bunch of great connections.
It's way more fun than doing tests
or spelling-word corrections.

Like, when I read a book on cows,
I thought of cool ice cream.
And when I thought of Brussels sprouts,
I thought that I might scream.

Of course, my strong connecting brain
came up with many others.
When someone mentioned stinky cheese,
I thought about my brothers.

In math, we studied triangles,
and pizza came to mind.
A square became a brownie—
the double-chocolate kind.

Some circles made me quickly think
of burgers on a plate.
From that point on, connections stopped—
I couldn't concentrate.

The hungry train inside my brain
had driven off the track.
Next time I'll save connecting things
till after I've had snack.

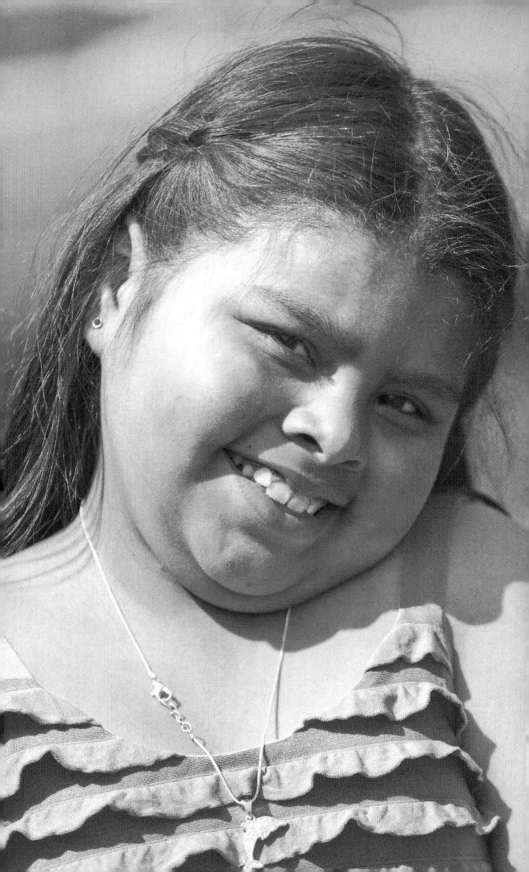

## I Predict

Our teacher stops our story time
and asks us to predict.
I try to guess what's coming next,
and sometimes I get picked.

I'm pretty good at doing it,
and often I am right.
Like, I predict that later on
today will be tonight.

I predict that two plus two
will always equal four.
And I'm completely confident
my dad will always snore.

I predict the sun will rise
and winter will bring ice.
And I predict, for my whole life,
my brother won't be nice.

I predict that stars will shine
and milk will come from cows.
And I predict, with certainty,
this poem will end right now.

## my pome iz purfekt

my pome iz purfekt
in evry way.
i ve siad al the wurds
that i neeeded to say.

rerite it? revue it?
im sory. i wont.
secund dratf riting?
not me. i just dont.

sumday i ll bee fameus.
my fans wil bee yeling
with praze for my rimes and
my fabulus speling.

# Equal

In math today, I listened hard
and did the best I could.
We talked about what *equal* means,
and then I understood.

Equal is when three is three,
and two's a twin with two.
Since you and I are six years old,
then I'm equal to you.

A dog is equal to friendship,
and summer is equal to fun.
Emergencies are equal
to calling 911.

Ice cream is equal to happiness,
and splinters are equal to pain.
And my brother's always equal to
a stinky knucklebrain.

## One Is Fun

My favorite number?
It is one.
One is all
I need for fun.

To me it's clear
that one is best—
a mile high
above the rest.

One's the peak—
the tippy-top.
Why count higher?
I just stop.

Bigger numbers
cannot hide
that they have tons
of ones inside.

Yes, one's enough.
It's always true.
(Except with cookies—
*one* won't do.)

## I'm Feeling Like a Cloud Today

I'm feeling like
a cloud today—
a little floaty
and very gray.

The sky above me
might be blue,
but I'm not letting
any through.

I'm not so windy
I'd complain,
but if you raise your voice at me,
I'll rain.

## You May Not Read This Poem
## If You're Taller Than This Line

When you are short, I can report,
it's not a lot of laughs.
You feel like you're a guinea pig
surrounded by giraffes.

Though I have learned to tolerate
my lower elevation,
when I am teased, I do not have
a wild celebration.

At some amusement parks, I find
I cannot ride a ride.
Because I am not tall enough,
I get disqualified.

So, I have made a simple rule—
I hope you saw my sign.
You may not read this poem if
you're taller than this line!

31

## Bellysmurp

If you're in school and feeling low,
here's a word you need to know:

It's *bellysmurp!*

I say it several times a day—
it seems to zoom my gloom away.

Say *bellysmurp!*

It also works when I am mad.
It never fails to make me glad.

Yes, *bellysmurp!*

If you are feeling kind of glum,
just toot your horn, and bang your drum.

Yell *bellysmurp!*

Repeat that word without a stop
until your teacher blows her top.

Shout *bellysmurp!*

It makes a rotten day a dream,
and always helps me let off steam.

(But *please* don't shout it now—I'll scream.)

# Dear Mom...

I'm writing from the belly
of a big blue whale.
I started in his mouth, of course,
but now I'm near his tail.

I brought a pad and pencil,
so I'm dropping you a line.
It's very dark and squishy here,
but otherwise it's fine.

My class went on a field trip
to see the salty sea.
When I fell in, I had to grin—
this creature swallowed me.

He seems to be a friendly sort—
at least he is inside.
I guess he simply wanted
to take me for a ride.

I'm dancing in his tummy now,
and I've begun to shout.
I'm pretty sure he'll throw up soon,
and I'll come flying out.

I should be home by dinner time,
so I'll be good and ready
for a boatload and a throatload
of your yummiest spaghetti.

If you were here, you might agree
my day has been exciting.
It goes to show what we both know:
I love creative writing!

# My Special Yellow Stick

I've brought this special yellow stick
for sharing time today.
It comes from times of long ago—
and just a block away.

I found it in my father's desk
and asked him what it was.
He sat me down to demonstrate
exactly what it does.

He took this stick and made it sharp
inside a loud machine.
It growled and spun in funny ways
I'd never heard or seen.

My dad then showed me something cool,
but first he turned a light on.
He took some stuff called "paper"
the yellow stick can write on!

He called this stick a "pencil"
and made it dance around.
It swirled and twirled to make some words,
without a lot of sound.

I know it seems a little weird
and primitive and slow,
but that's the way they wrote stuff out
a zillion years ago.

## What Happened to My Snack as My Mom Dropped Me Off at School

*(Sing to the tune of "Twinkle, Twinkle Little Star")*

Wrinkled, crinkled candy bar
got run over by a car.
Once you were so round and sweet—
now you're flattened in the street.
Though you're gross and greasy-gray,
I will eat you anyway.

## Sorryness

My heart is filled with sorryness
for what I said to you.
My words were filled with angryness,
but none of them were true.

If I were you, I'm sure I'd feel
a mountain of annoyness.
So, let's go back to being friends
and sharing smiles of joyness.

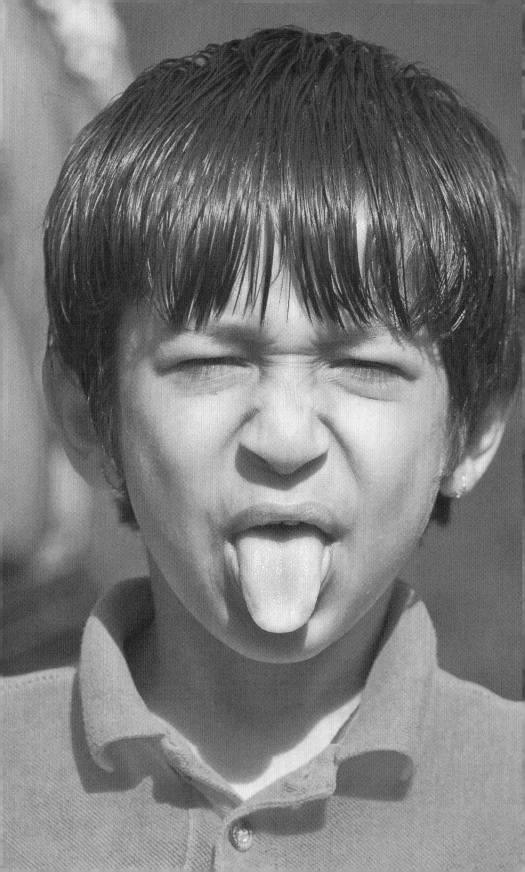

# Don't Call My Teacher "Nice"

Don't *ever* call my teacher "nice."
She doesn't quite deserve it.
Come in someday and watch her work,
and we can both observe it.

"Nice" will never work for her,
when better words will do.
In fact, I've made a list right here
of more than just a few.

She isn't nice—she's fabulous
and marvelous and great.
She's totally incredible,
as she will demonstrate.

Her manner is stupendous.
She's quick and kind and smart.
She makes us feel like we're the best
at everything we start.

So, please don't ever call her "nice"—
the word is dull and flat.
She's just the super-est teacher there is,
and *that* is simply *that*.

## I'm Too Busy to Finish This P____

I'm sorry, I'm too busy.
I cannot find the time
to search and find another word
to make this poem _____.

I'm dashing extra fast today,
so I have got a hunch
that I will need to ask you, please,
if you could eat my _____.

I'm glad I have a friend like you
who's totally goodhearted,
so you can step into my shoes
and finish what I've _____.

Since I can always count on you,
I think it would be best
if you would sit for just a sec
and take my spelling _____.

# I'm Staying Here

I have a brief announcement—
I'd like to make it clear:
I'm staying here in second grade
for more than just this year.

I love it here, I'm pleased to say.
And though it may sound strange,
I know inside I've hit my stride,
and I don't need to change.

My teacher's style makes me smile—
she's strict, but kind and funny.
So, I will *never* leave this place.
I'm like a bear with honey.

There's awesome science stuff to do
and books I love to read.
The writing is exciting,
and the math is just my speed.

Besides, those bossy third-grade kids
are way too big and tough.
I saw them out at recess,
and they play a little rough.

Hooray, hooray for second grade!
I need to shout and cheer!
It's cool to think in twenty years
that I will still be here.

## Best Friends Forever

I will not tell a lie to you—
on that you can depend.
I'm super proud to say out loud
you are my finest friend.

You never fight, your smile is bright,
your jokes are clearly clever.
And if you share your snack with me,
we'll be best friends forever.

## What I Told My Teacher When the Juice Spilled All Over the Table, Across the Floor, and Out the Door

I took the juice you gave me, ma'am,
and poured it carefully.
But something happened near the end,
quite unexpectedly.

I guess my very thirsty throat
just told my hand to pour
and pour and pour and pour and pour
and pour a little more.

And now I see a stream of juice
is trickling down the hall.
I think the glass you gave me, ma'am,
was just a bit too small.

## Ouch

I learned a lesson
yesterday
that only
experience brings:
When you're waiting
for your turn,
don't stand
in front of swings.

## My Pocket Poem

I have the coolest poem
in my pocket for today.
Its style makes me smile
in a bright and bouncy way.

It's hiding there with my favorite rock,
and a dusty key to a rusty lock,
a purple crayon broke in two,
and a fraying lace to a stinky shoe,
the quarter I will need for snack,
and a shiny ball with a tiny crack,
two blue jay feathers I just found,
and worms and dirt from in the ground,
a busted wheel from a model car,
and half a chocolate candy bar.

I know my poem's in there
because my fingers felt it.
But I'm a little worried now...
the candy bar just melted.

# I Got a Hundred Points

In school, I got a *hundred* points
for being extra nice.
And then I got a *hundred* more
for being nice twice.

At snack, I got a *thousand*,
but I did not relax.
By lunch, I had a *million* more
for many thoughtful acts.

When I got home, I told my mom,
and she was quite excited.
So, who awarded all those points?
I'm pleased to say that *I* did!

# Hooray for PJ Day

Let's bang the drum! At last it's come!
Pajama Day is here!
The finest, funnest, number-one-est
day we have all year!

Pajamas are the rule today
for every kid and grownup.
A fine display of bedtimewear
has positively shown up.

The teachers and the office folks,
are wearing jammies, too.
The lunchroom ladies have theirs on,
as do the cleaning crew.

Of all the PJs I have seen,
the principal's are best.
He's got a yellow sleep suit on
with hearts across his chest.

I saw him through his office door,
slouching in his chair.
His eyes were closed, and in his arms
he hugged his teddy bear.

I'd scream, "Hooray for PJ Day!"
with all my lungs and heart,
but waking up the principal
would not be very smart.

# I Used Them All

I've got my Yellow, got my Red,
my Black, and Tan, and Blue.
My Brown is here, and Violet,
and Pink Flamingo, too.

Here's Burnt Sienna, Olive Green,
Periwinkle, Peach,
Gold, and Silver, Bittersweet,
and Melon—one of each.

I've used Maroon, and Lavender,
and Plum, and Tangerine.
And here's Banana Mania,
and Caribbean Green.

I really love Outrageous Orange,
and, yes, here's Razzmatazz.
Ah, Mango Tango, Outer Space,
and Purply Pizzazz.

I'll add some Hot Magenta here,
and Orchid, just for fun.
And finally some Manatee,
and Fern—and now I'm done.

My teacher will be proud of me
that I could use them all
to draw this crayon dinosaur
across our classroom wall.

## Who Needs Recess?

They took our recess time away
so we can study more.
We practice stuff that's on the tests
to get a higher score.

We barely even stop for snack—
there isn't time to do it.
We've got important work to do
and need to hurry through it.

Besides, who needs a recess break?
Who needs to jump and run?
To be as smart as we can be,
who needs to see the sun?

Who needs to play a silly game?
Who needs to breathe fresh air?
Who needs to feel the wild wind
whooshing through her hair?

I need to get my highest score,
and I will always try to.
So, who needs recess, anyway?

*I'm pretty sure that I do.*

# My Teacher Is So Weird

I have a cat named Puppy Dog.
My doggie's name is Kitty.
Lady is my guinea pig,
and he is very pretty.

I named my goldfish Bluebird.
My parrot goes by Fishy.
I even have a favorite rock—
he loves his nickname, Squishy.

My horse, of course, is Bumblebee.
My chicken's name is Pig.
My mouse is extra happy when
I call him Mr. Big.

My brother's name is Nancy.
My sister's simply Tom.
I call my mother Daddy,
and my father's always Mom.

My teacher brought a rabbit in,
and, just as I had feared,
she named our bunny Cottontail—
my teacher is so weird!

## What I Decided about Goldilocks during Storytime

Goldilocks, it seems to me,
was whiny, rude, and bratty.
If I behaved that way today,
I'd hear it from my daddy.

My mom would quickly rush to take
some privileges away.
But Goldilocks got none of that—
she simply ran away.

I think those bears were generous
and couldn't be much sweeter,
but given all the stuff she broke,
I was surprised when Goldie woke
the bears did not just eat her.

# I Never Count

When it comes to numbers,
I am a counting star.
But I am careful not to count
while riding in a car.

I do not count in classrooms,
in libraries, or halls.
I never like to count amounts
of recess bouncy balls.

I barely mention numbers
while up or downing stairs.
I rarely find the time to count
while standing or in chairs.

I cannot count in closets,
in basements, or a bed.
I hate to count in bathrooms
or even in my head.

But when I'm eating breakfast,
that's when I count the best.
I'm just a kitchen counter,
as you have surely guessed.

# Someday I'll Be a Teacher

When I grow up, I think I'll be
a teacher at my school.
I'll be the kind that kids will find
to be extremely cool.

I've watched my teachers carefully.
I've seen the stuff they do.
And I'm completely confident
that I could do it, too.

I'm super great at helping kids,
like teachers do all day.
And all the things they say to us
are things that I can say.

I'm smart enough to answer kids
whenever they don't know stuff.
And I'd be sure the kids I'd teach
would never try to throw stuff.

I like to chat with grownups.
I'm great at writing notes.
I'm awesome cleaning sinks and floors
and hanging winter coats.

I would not sleep at meetings
and never would be mean.
And I'm the best of all my friends
at keeping whiteboards clean.

I know I have the skills I need
to do it easily.
And I'll be sure the kids I teach
are perfect—just like me!

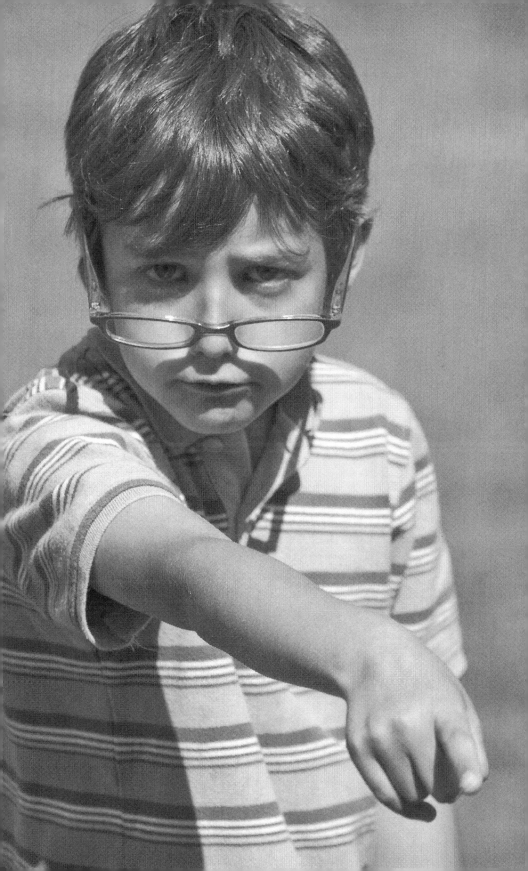

## I'm Absolutely Certain

I'm certain! I'm certain!
I absolutely know.
Please call on me and you will see
that I'm a total pro.

I'm positively positive—
as certain as the sun.
If you are looking for the truth,
my answer is the one.

My explanation's awesome
and needs a special mention.
I know that other hands are up,
but mine deserves attention.

I've worked it out, without a doubt.
My voice is sure and strong.
I'm absolutely certain that
I'm absolutely *wrong*!

# My Pencil Stinks at Spelling

My pencil stinks at spelling,
no matter how I use it.
If there's a way to write words wrong,
my pencil seems to choose it.

It never knows the order when
it comes to *e*'s and *i*'s.
It always puts them backward,
no matter which it tries.

When turning *y* words plural,
it makes a mighty mess.
It never can remember
to change to *i-e-s*.

For *ph* words, it puts an *f*,
and *e*'s where *y*'s should go.
I'm sorry—these are spelling rules
a pencil ought to know.

I've noticed my eraser
is also not too bright.
It sometimes wipes away a word
that's spelled exactly right.

My only hope for spelling now,
as words get long and harder,
is writing them in pen with ink—
I hope my pen is smarter.

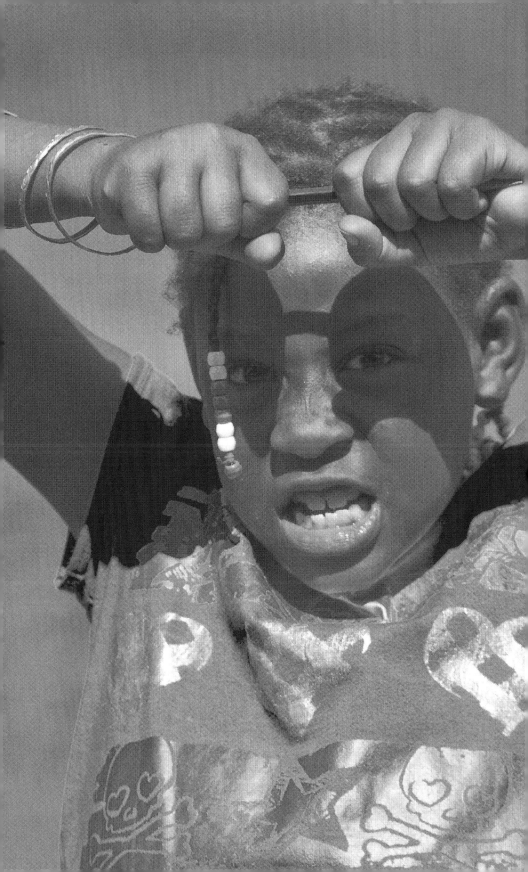

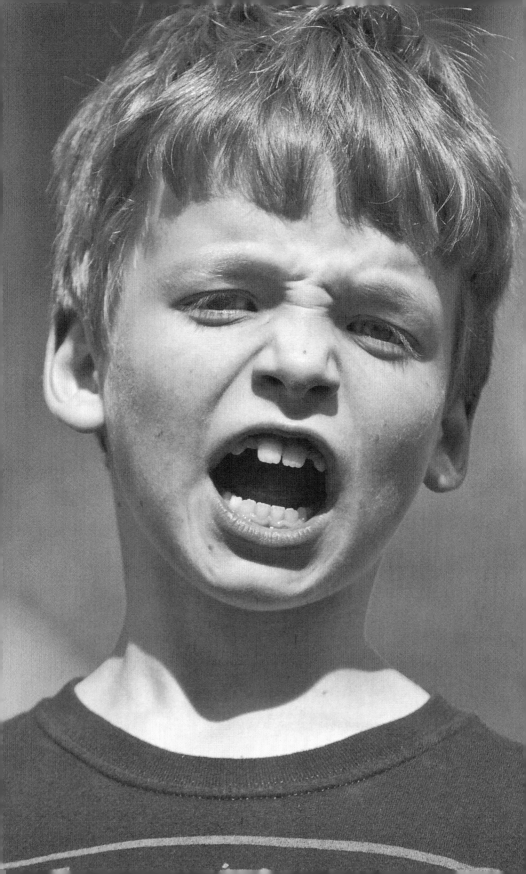

## I'm So Much Better

Today we had a test in gym—
we climbed and rolled,
and dashed and vaulted,
jumped and pumped,
and somersaulted,
turned and twisted,
flexed and flopped,
slipped and slid,
and never stopped—
and it was *super hard.*

I told the PE teacher,
"I climb and roll,
and dash and vault,
jump and pump,
and somersault,
turn and twist,
flex and flop,
slip and slide,
*much better*
when I'm in *my* backyard."

## Our Hundredth Day

Today's our hundredth day of school,
and I could hardly wait
to share the hundred things I brought
to help us celebrate.

I had a hundred jelly beans
of every brilliant hue,
but on the bus they looked so good,
I sort of ate a few.

My hundred yummy chocolate drops
might be a great success—
until they melted in my pants
and made one chocolate mess.

My backup was some cheesy chips
from our convenience store.
But then my brother sat on them
and made two thousand more.

Through my tears, I somehow found
the perfect thing to share:
A hundred short and soggy sobs
came floating through the air.

# Who Needs Numbers?

Who needs numbers?
I sure don't.
Ask me to use 'em?
Sorry, I won't.

Numbers are silly—
a waste of my time.
They're never as fun as
a poem with rhyme.

They're useless and boring
in any amount.
Letters and words
are all that should count.

You need some more reasons
why numbers aren't great?
I bet I could give you
one hundred and eight!

## We Speak Friend

A new kid joined our class today.
He talks in Japanese.
Another boy speaks Arabic,
with different ABCs.

Two sets of twins speak Spanish,
with words that float like feathers.
It sounds to me like harmony
when they are all together.

I'm fairly sure a Chinese girl
just asked if she could play.
But none of us could understand
the words she had to say.

Although we didn't talk a lot,
we had a bunch of fun.
We raced and ran, without a plan,
beneath the recess sun.

When we all meet tomorrow,
I know we can depend
that we will all communicate
by simply speaking Friend.

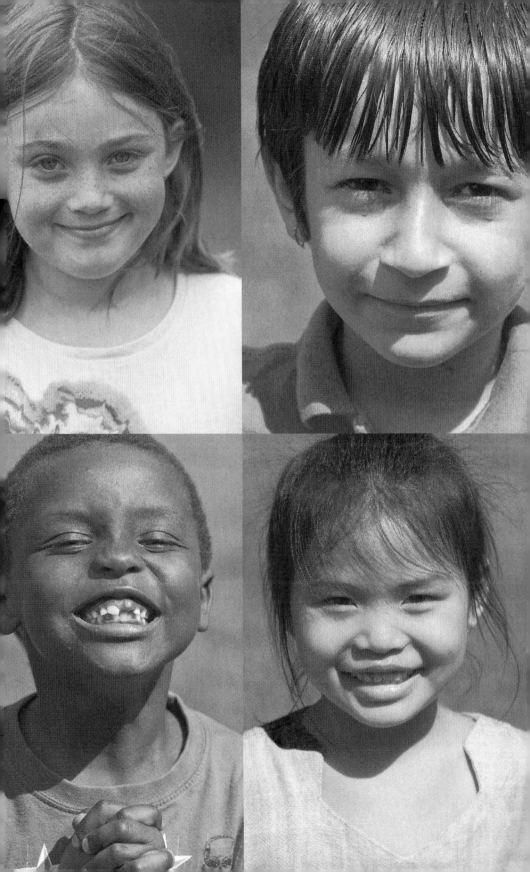

# My Weather Report

Today I am the weatherman,
so here is my report.
I'll try to cover everything,
but also keep it short.

Watching skies takes careful eyes.
It's fun, but never funny.
So, I will say the sun today
will be extremely sunny.

The clouds will all be cloudy.
The heat will be quite hot.
Some chilly air will cool us off—
except when it will not.

All raindrops will be rainy,
and mostly they'll be wet.
And if it snows, the flakes will be
as white as they can get.

The temperature, I'm pretty sure,
will be exactly right
and stay that way throughout the day
and mostly through the night.

Some stars will fill the evening sky,
like lots of tiny sparks.
And one last thing that you should know—
the darkness will be dark.

## Why My Desk Is in the Hall

I'm loopy for learning.
I'm nutty for school.
I'm thrilled that my teacher
is totally cool.

I'm nuts about music,
computers, and art.
I hardly can wait for
each school day to start.

I'm crazy for science
and writing and reading.
I even do math down at lunch
while I'm eating!

I'm perfectly nutty
for *everything* there:
my friends and my pencils,
my desk and my chair.

But I have a problem
I simply can't hide:
Our class is "nut free,"
so I can't go inside.

# My Pencil Is a Rocket Ship

My pencil is a rocket ship
that zooms me to the moon.
And often it's a piccolo
that whistles me a tune.

At times it is a telephone
that jingles near my ear.
Its sound, I've found, is soft enough
so only I can hear.

My pencil is a magic wand,
performing tricks for me.
Its smoke and blasts are lightning fast,
and only I can see.

When it becomes a drumstick
and builds a bouncy beat,
it bumps and dances in my hand
and tickles toes and feet.

My pencil is a silver sword
that shimmers with surprise,
quieting a dragon's roar.
(But never near his eyes.)

I love to use my pencil as
a bold and bright baton
that players in my orchestra
can all depend upon.

But when my pencil's penciling,
it fills me with delight.
We work together, hand in hand,
on poems that we write.

## Who Cleans the Whiteboard This Week?

Monday can be Frankie's day,
and Tuesday is for Sue.
Wednesday is Rebecca's,
and Thursday is for you.
Friday will be Bobby's,
and it should be just fine
if Saturday and Sunday
are absolutely mine.

## I Got the Answer

I finally got the answer!
I knew that it would come.
I worked it out all by myself.
I knew I wasn't dumb!

My teacher will be proud to see
I triumphed in my quest.
And even though my answer's great,
sadly, it's a little late.
I could have used it *yesterday*
on my subtraction test.

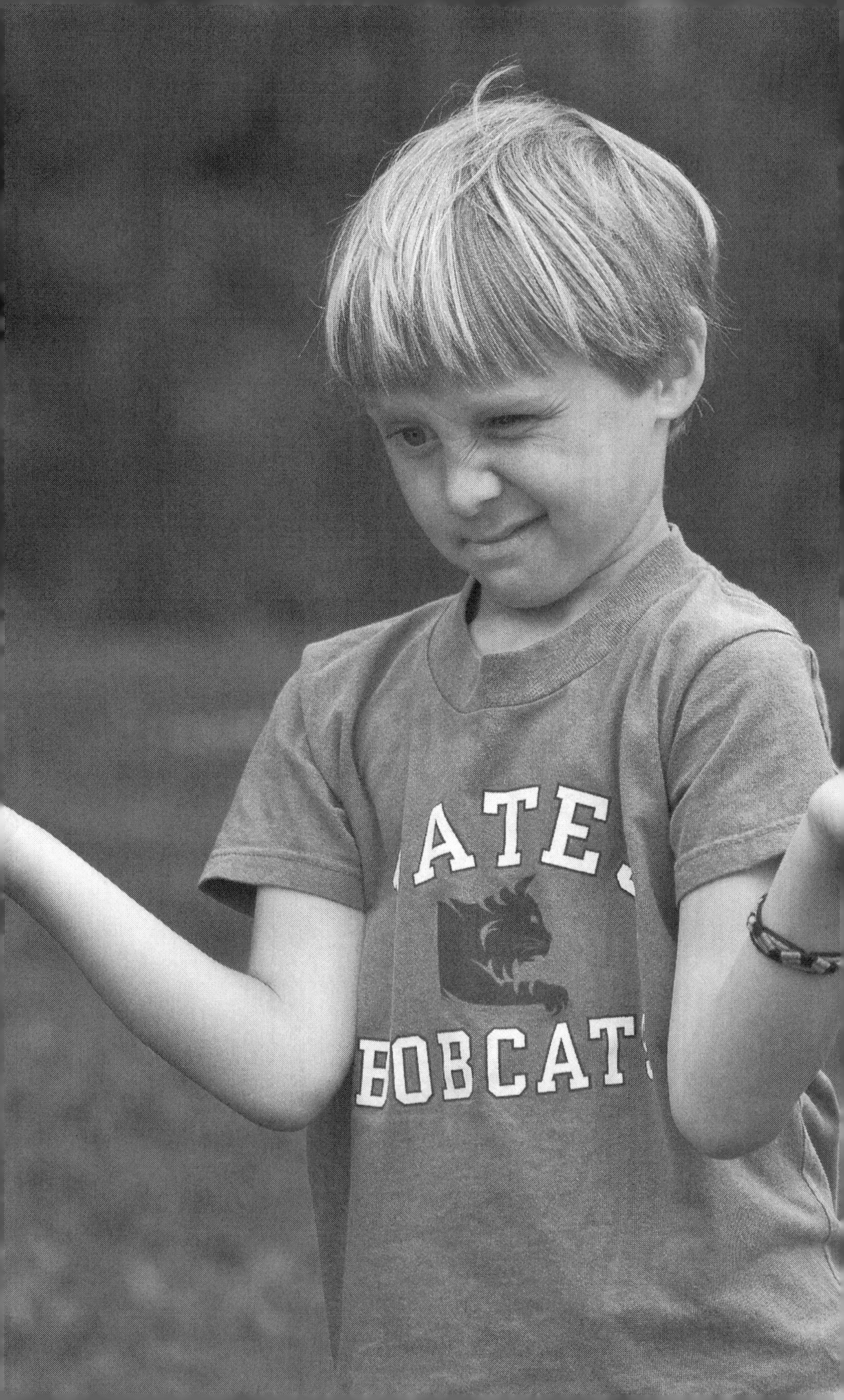

# Teaching My Sister

Counting is my favorite thing
of all the things I do.
I want to teach my sister,
so she can do it, too.

I made some simple rhymes to use
to help her get it right.
My sister's pretty little,
and she's really not too bright.

*One, two,*
*four, five,*
*eighty-three.*
*I know you*
*can count on me!*
*Five, six,*
*nine, ten,*
*fifty-two.*
*I hope I*
*can count on you!*

She's looking at me funny now
and showing some concern.
When it comes to counting right,
she'll prob'ly never learn.

## My Backpack Is Bursting

My backpack is bursting
with all of my stuff.
It seems to be growing—
it can't eat enough.

It swallowed my homework,
my jacket, my snack.
It seems to devour
each thing that I pack.

And down in that darkness
where everything's swelling,
I just heard a burp—
and now something is smelling.

But that's how I love it—
so messy, it's scary.
Who cares if it's nearly
too heavy to carry?

# Our Pumpkin Farm Field Trip

All the pumpkins in the field
have very different names.
One might be Penelope,
and one, I bet, is James.

One is Harry, one is Hailey.
There is Owen, Mike, and Bailey.
I see one that looks like Mia,
then there's Ryan and Sophia.

On the right are Seth and Nick,
Lauren, Lilly—take your pick.
This group here is Isabella,
Tyler, Jason, Peg, and Ella.

Others might be Hank or Hannah,
Colin, John, or Julianna.
Jenny, Robin, Jacob, Dylan—
all the names that you can fill in.

Some are Claire or Mary.
Still more are Luke and Mac.
But when they're carved and make the scene,
all brightly lit for Halloween,
they change their names to Jack.

## Spelling Star

I spelled a bunch of words today
when it was time to write.
My pencil flew across the page
in supersonic flight.

I'll take my writer's notebook home
and do some more tonight.
And when I spell those words again,
I bet I'll spell them *right*!

# The Mighty *Er*

An *er* is mostly boring—
a simple, wimpy sound.
But sometimes humble *er*'s can be
the strongest sound around.

*Er*'s can hang at ends of words,
like little train cabooses.
That's where they work their magic tricks
and show their many uses.

An *er* can quickly make a word
quite different than before.
I have a few examples here—
I bet you know some more.

*Er* makes *fast* much *faster*
and helps things *tall* get *taller*.
Some *quiet* things get *quieter*,
and *small* things grow much *smaller*.

A noise that's *loud* gets *louder* fast,
and something *short* gets *shorter*.
An *er* can turn some *quarts* of juice,
like magic, into *quarters*!

An *er* can be a trickster, too,
when *broth* becomes my *brother*.
And late at night, around a light,
a *moth* becomes my *mother*!

Though *er*'s are mostly fun to add,
some *hard* things do get *harder*.
And *er*'s will show the wordy world
you're not just *smart*—you're *smarter*!

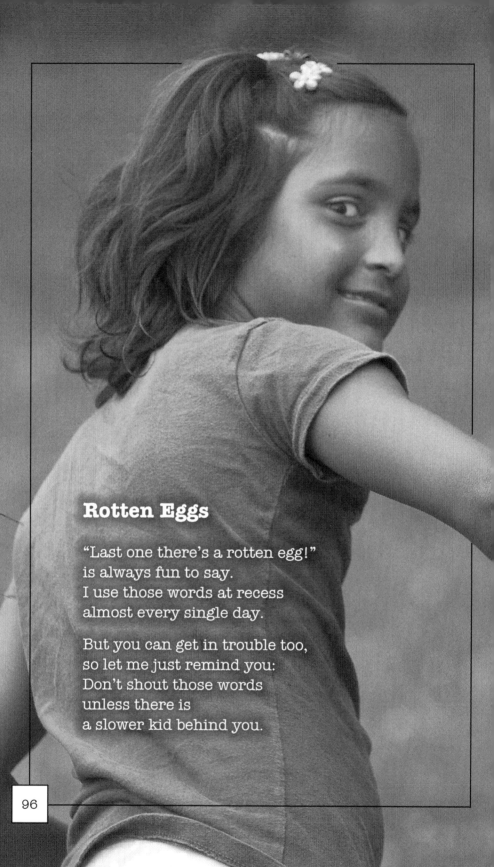

## Rotten Eggs

"Last one there's a rotten egg!"
is always fun to say.
I use those words at recess
almost every single day.

But you can get in trouble too,
so let me just remind you:
Don't shout those words
unless there is
a slower kid behind you.

# I'm Number One!

I drink a *lot* of water
each day when I'm in class.
So, I'm the champ at reaching for
our classroom's bathroom pass.

We never have to raise our hands,
'cause everybody knows
if someone's body has to *go*,
then someone's body goes.

So, guzzle water every day.
It's healthy and it's fun.
And maybe you (like me) will be
your classroom's number one.

# I've Brought a Guest to School Today

I've brought a guest to school today—
he's standing by my chair.
I know he looks surprising,
but I wish you wouldn't stare.

Although his hair's a little long
and he has tiny feet,
he's just about the nicest guy
you'd ever want to meet.

He doesn't speak our language,
but seems to understand.
He's pretty shy and quiet,
but he'd love to shake your hand.

He loves to learn and mostly does
exactly what he's told.
It's really quite amazing
since he isn't very old.

He's handsome as a movie star—
his eyebrows to his toes.
It doesn't seem to matter that
he isn't wearing clothes.

Our teacher hasn't seen him yet,
but they'll be meeting soon.
I hope she will agree to let
him stay all afternoon.

The problem is, for him to stay,
we'd have to break a rule:
I'm pretty sure a puppy dog
is not allowed in school.

## I'm Going to Be a Star

I'm going to be a star someday—
the world will know my face.
I'll be the cause of dreams and screams
from here to outer space.

My smile will be *everywhere*,
beneath my famous eyes.
My face will be more popular
than chocolate shakes and fries.

It's not for lots of money that
I seek a life of fame.
It's mostly so that teachers won't
mispronounce my name.

## Happy Birthdays to Me!

I found my birth certificate,
and I was pleased to see
that Monday was the day the world
was introduced to me.

So every Monday I announce
to everyone who's near me
that they can give me lots of gifts
and sing to me and cheer me.

I get to wear the Birthday Crown
and claim the Birthday Seat.
And then, at snack, I always share
my special birthday treat.

My teacher isn't tickled,
but there's nothing she can do.
See, I don't have *one* birthday now—
I've got *fifty-two*!

# See You Later, Refrigerator

*(A Goodbye Poem for Two Very Silly Friends)*

Bye - Bye , French Fry .

Gotta go , cookie dough .

See you later , refrigerator .

In a while , pancake pile .

Adiós , pot roast .

Keep it real , banana peel .

Toodeloo , barbecue .

Have to run , hot dog bun .

Be good , Robin Hood .

So long , King Kong .

See you soon , Daniel Boone .

Good day , Milky Way .

Time to hop , carrot top .

Don't go far , candy bar .

Take care , grizzly bear .

Pleasant trip , paper clip .

Out the door , dinosaur .

Farewell , caramel .

# Thanks to a Good-Looking Bunch of Smarties!

Journey     Livia     Hayden     Helen

Noah     Clare     Priya     Stirling

Katy     Chloe     Wren     Baxter

Isabel     Alex     Dylan     Zelda

Rubin

Miles

Theo

Uma

Cora

Shaun

Joshua

Ali

Abdulhakh

Joscelyn

Ashlin

Mo'najah

Paw Bwe

Pete, Ted, & Win

# Ted Scheu (That Poetry Guy)

Fifteen years ago, a very smart first grader gave Ted his nickname, and it stuck. Fortunately Ted has stuck with writing poetry for kids and with kids! He absolutely loves that he gets to be a kid every day, in his poems and in his visits to schools around the globe—traveling from his home in Middlebury, Vermont. When he's not writing honest, humorous poems, Ted loves to ride his bike and play with friends—just like any kid his age. His poems are published widely in anthologies in the US (Philomel, Scholastic, and Meadowbrook Press), in the UK (Macmillan, Scholastic, and Hodder), and in his other collections, *I Froze My Mother*, *I Tickled My Teachers*, and *I Threw My Brother Out*—all from Young Poets' Press. Learn much more about Ted at his web site: **www.poetryguy.com**.

# Peter Lourie

Pete is an adventurer, photographer, anthropologist and teacher—and as if that's not enough, he is also a celebrated children's author. In his many award-winning books, Pete takes us to some of the most remote and rugged regions of the world including the Amazon, the Arctic, and every-where wild in between. He just got back from somewhere "in between"—working at high altitude in Cuzco, Peru on a new book for kids. He also makes tons of visits to schools around the world each year—helping kids (and teachers) get excited about writing, reading and adventuring. Learn more about him at his web site **www.peterlourie.com**. When he's not traveling, Pete lives happily in Weybridge, Vermont.

# Winslow Colwell

Winslow Colwell is a true man for all seasons, who also hap-pens to be a marvelous designer of books, kites, and pretty much all things designable, printable, and buildable—many of which may be found at his web site at **www.wcolwell.com**. When he's not using his magical powers to design things like this book, he loves to dance and play with his wife and daughter, take photos of things from funny angles, and play his guitar. Win lives in East Middlebury, Vermont.

# Need more copies of
## *Now I Know My ZBCs*
# for your favorite teachers, classmates and family?

### Here are four fabulous ways:

**1.** For super-speedy delivery, go to Ted's web site at **www.poetryguy.com** and push the "Order Books!" link, and you will be zoomed right to the publisher.

**2.** Or you can print out an order form at Ted's web site at **www.poetryguy.com**, then snail-mail it to Ted. If you order a book directly from Ted, he can sign the books for you. When you order, please let him know exactly how you'd like him to inscribe them. As the form will explain, send a check by mail for $12.95 (US$) for each book to Ted Scheu, PO Box 564, Middlebury, VT 05753, USA. Please include $3.00 (US) for postage and handling for up to four books, and $3.00 for each four books after that. To order from outside the US, go to #1 above.

**3.** Or you can surf right over to **amazon.com** or **barnesandnoble.com** and order the book there.

**4.** Best of all, politely ask your wonderful local book store to order the book for you!

## Thanks!

"Ted Scheu is the poetry guy.
  He'll make you all laugh
  And laugh till you cry.
  His humor is wry and dry by-and-by.
  So please give this poetry guy a good try."

**— Douglas Florian**
author of a multitude of delicious
collections of poetry for kids, including
*Poetrees, insectlopedia,* and *Bing Bang Boing*

54449373R00063

Made in the USA
Columbia, SC
31 March 2019